Friends Around the World

Written by Ana Galan

Acknowledgments

The publisher would like to thank the following for their kind permission to reproduce their photographs:
(Key: b-bottom; c-center; l-left; r-right; t-top)
123RF.com: Dennis Peppin 18br, ErickN 7tr, Joshua Resnick 4bl, 6tl, 14tl, 22tl, 30tl, Lisa Strachan 13tl; **Alamy Images:** Agencja Fotograficzna Caro 6bl, Anne- Marie Palmer 24b, Bill Bachman 13br, 20br, blickwinkel / McPHOTO / SBA 4tc, 10tr, 18tl, 26tl, Bushpilot 10br, 30br, Carson Ganci 15tr, Chad McDermott 14-15, David Hancock 21br, DP RF 26b, Esa Hitula 27bl, Glyn Thomas 11tl, Götz C. Glaser 8-9, Greg Balfour Evans 16b, James Allen 23- cr, Karen Appleyard 29bl, Patrick Ward 28-29t, PCN Black 14bl, Prisma / Raga Jose Fuste 9b, Steve Vidler 8bl; **Creatas:** 19tl; **Shutterstock.com:** Banana Republic Images 16-17, Bob Deneizen 28b, Horse Crazy 5tr, 12tl, 20tl, 28tl, karrapavan 26-27, Kirk Geisler 19, Leah Kennedy 20-21, 3lt, Maalke van Besian 12-13, Mark van Vuren 24-25, 3lb, Mikadun 10-11, Mirko Sobotta 17b, Songquan Deng 6-7, 22-23, Tom Wang 5br, 8tl, 16tl, 24tl

Cover images: *Front:* **Alamy Images:** blickwinkel / McPHOTO / SBA; *Back:* **Alamy Images:** Sergey Borisov

All other images © Pearson Education

Every effort has been made to trace the copyright holders and we apologize in advance for any unintentional omissions. We would be pleased to insert the appropriate acknowledgment in any subsequent edition of this publication.

ISBN-13: 978-0-328-83280-4
ISBN-10: 0-328-83280-4

5   16

Contents

Today my teacher, Miss Thomson, gave us a great surprise. We will exchange e-mails, letters, and pictures with our new friends from around the world!

Miss Thomson gave me the names of my new e-pals. I found out some facts about where they live.

My e-pals live far away!

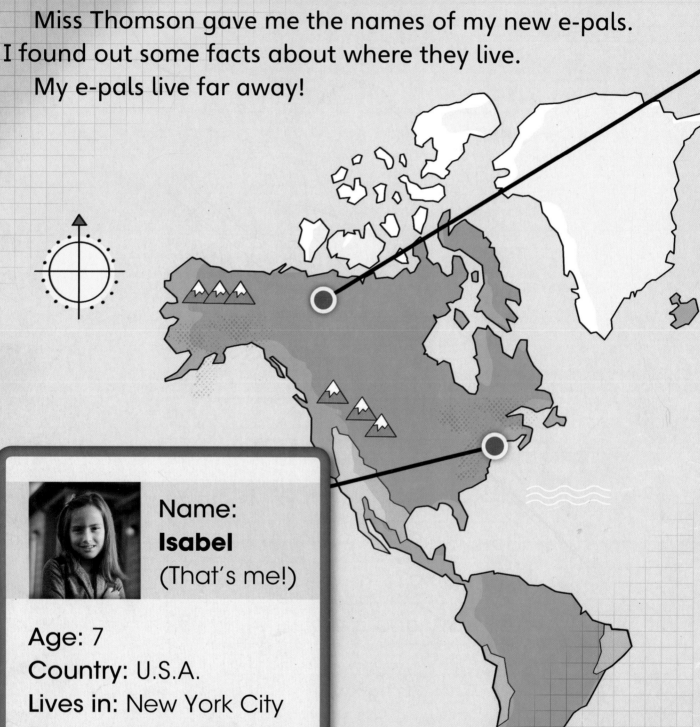

Name:
Isabel
(That's me!)

Age: 7
Country: U.S.A.
Lives in: New York City
Type of place: Big city

Name:
Akiak

Age: 8
Country: Canada
Lives in: Yellowknife
Type of place: Small city

Name:
Dan

Age: 8
Country: Australia
Lives in:
Northern Territory
Type of place:
Remote farm

Name:
Hau

Age: 7
Country: Vietnam
Lives in: Ho Chi Minh City
Type of place: Big city

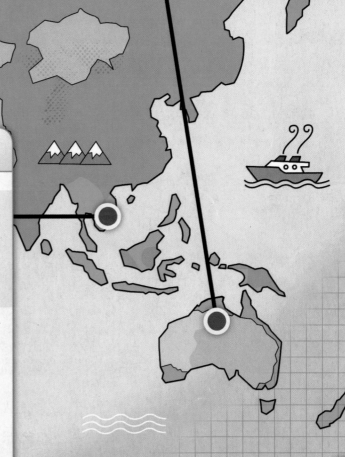

Isabel
New York City, U.S.A.
To: Hau, Akiak, Dan

Dear friends,

My name is Isabel. I'm seven years old. I live in New York City, in the United States of America. I live on the 14th floor of a big apartment building. Don't worry—there's an elevator!

I take the subway to school with my mom. The subway is an underground train. Here are some pictures of my city. How do you go to school?

Please write back soon!

Your new e-pal,
Isabel

The subway is a fast way to get around the city.

The Statue of Liberty is very famous.

This tall building is called the Empire State Building. It is 103 floors high!

Hau
Ho Chi Minh City, Vietnam
To: Isabel

Hi, Isabel,

My name is Hau. I'm seven years old. I live in Ho Chi Minh City in Vietnam. I speak Vietnamese and I'm learning English.

There are over five million motorcycles in my city! My mom takes me to school on her motorcycle. I wear a helmet and my school uniform. It's a white shirt, blue scarf, and blue skirt.

I hope you like my pictures.

Your friend,
Hau

Here's my family riding our motorcycle! People wear masks for protection from the smog.

Ho Chi Minh City is the largest city in Vietnam.

○ There are more motorcycles than cars in my city.

Akiak
Yellowknife, Canada
To: Isabel

Hi, Isabel!

My name is Akiak. It's an Inuit name meaning "brave." I speak English, French, and Inuktitut.

I live in the Arctic Circle. It's very cold here. I walk to school in a heavy parka, boots, and a warm hat. Sometimes I wear snowshoes!

Do you play any sports? I love to play ice hockey with my friends. I love snowboarding too!

Yours truly,
Akiak

Snowboarding is a popular sport here.

Here are some Canadian bills.

Snowmobiles help us move quickly across the snow.

Dan
Northern Territory, Australia
To: Isabel

Hi, Isabel,

My name is Dan. I live on a farm in the Australian outback. The closest town is Alice Springs. It is three hours away by car!

We have lots of animals on our farm. We have horses, cows, and chickens.

My sister and I go to the School of the Air. This means we don't go into school each day—it's too far. Our teacher uses the Internet to give us work. She visits us at home once a year. Each semester, she sends us school books, software, and DVDs.

I need to go feed the chickens now.

Talk to you soon!
Dan

Sometimes wild kangaroos come into our backyard!

Our farm is a long way from the nearest town!

Children and their parents can talk to teachers using the Internet.

Isabel
New York City, U.S.A.
To: Hau, Akiak, Dan

Dear friends,

Last weekend I went to a baseball game. My favorite team is the New York Yankees. When I go to a game, I always eat a hot dog!

I like sports. I play soccer in the fall. My coach told me that in most of the world, they call soccer "football"!

Here are some pictures of my favorite sports.

Write soon!
Isabel

American football is a lot of fun!

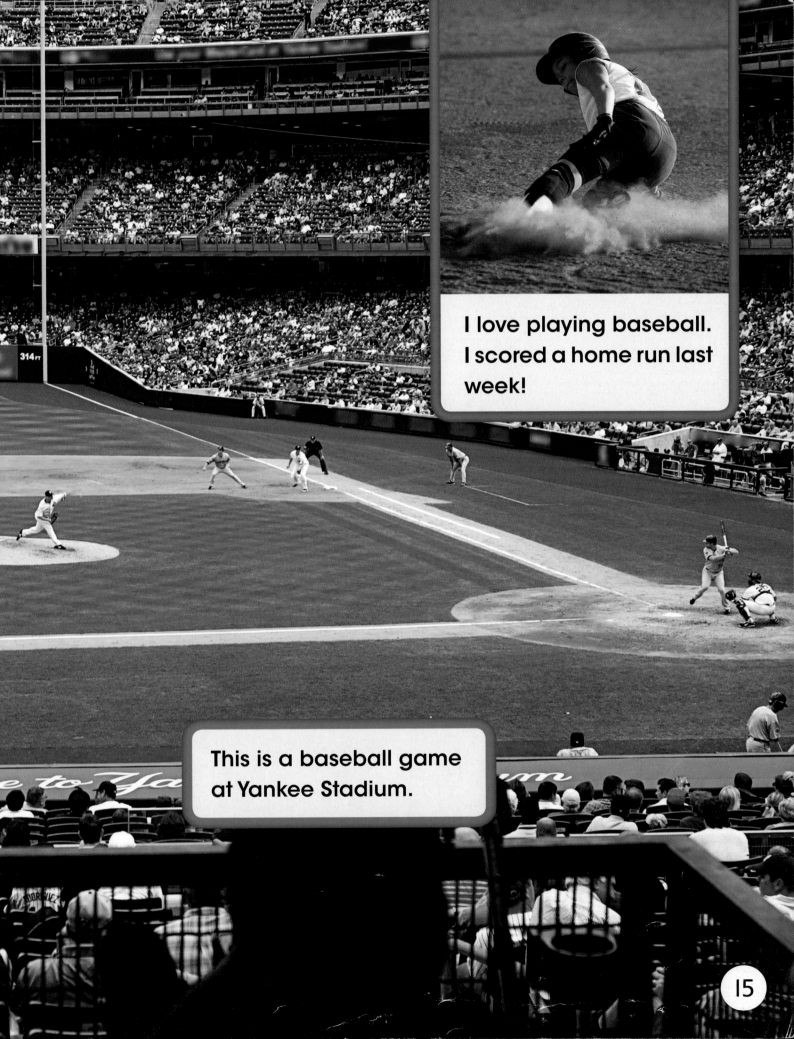

I love playing baseball. I scored a home run last week!

This is a baseball game at Yankee Stadium.

Hau
Ho Chi Minh City, Vietnam
To: Isabel

Hi, Isabel,

Today I took pictures of some of my favorite foods. There are many food markets in Ho Chi Minh City! There are street vendors selling food on almost every corner.

Some mornings I eat noodle soup for breakfast. It is yummy! I love fruit, especially dragon fruit. It's pink on the outside and white on the inside.

Your friend,
Hau

These people are selling fruit. They are wearing traditional Vietnamese hats.

Boats bring fruit and vegetables to the city.

This soup is called pho. It has noodles and vegetables.

Akiak
Yellowknife, Canada
To: Isabel

Hi, Isabel,

Guess what? My dad is teaching me to drive a dog sled! We have ten sled dogs. Every year there's a race in my town. My dad always competes. Maybe one day I will too.

Last weekend we went camping and ice fishing. The lake was frozen, so we drilled a hole in the ice. At night, we cooked the fish over the fire. We also ate my favorite meal—caribou!

I saw many animals—even an Arctic fox!

Yours truly,
Akiak

My grandfather caught a really big fish!

The Arctic fox is white in the winter and brown in the summer.

My dad takes part in dog sled races.

Dan
Northern Territory, Australia
To: Isabel

Hi, Isabel,

There are many fun things to do in the outback. I love to ride my horse. Sometimes I help to round up our cows. We ride our horses behind the cows to bring them home. It's a lot of fun. It can be dangerous, so I always wear a helmet!

On weekends I like to play backyard cricket with my sister.

Talk to you soon!
Dan

When it's winter in New York, it's summer in Australia!

Rounding up the cows is called a cattle drive.

You need a good bat to play cricket.

Isabel
New York City, U.S.A.
To: Hau, Akiak, Dan

Dear friends,

There is a lot to do in New York City too. We have lots of museums. My favorite is the Museum of Natural History. You can see real dinosaur skeletons there. They're enormous!

In the summer, I like to go to the beach. New York is by the ocean. In the winter, I like to go ice skating in Central Park.

We have four seasons—spring, summer, fall, and winter. What is the weather like where you live?

Your friend,
Isabel

There are lots of interesting things to see at the American Museum of Natural History!

I love going to Central Park in the winter.

Hau
Ho Chi Minh City, Vietnam
To: Isabel

Hi, Isabel,

It's always hot in Ho Chi Minh City! We have two seasons—rainy season and dry season. During the rainy season, it pours every day. Sometimes, the river overflows and floods the streets.

In the dry season, I love playing in the park. There are lots of great playgrounds!

Your friend,
Hau

○ **There are some great playgrounds in my city!**

The streets get flooded, but we still go out!

Akiak
Yellowknife, Canada
To: Isabel

Hi, Isabel,

There was a big blizzard in our town last week. We couldn't go to school for three days! I built a huge snow castle when it stopped snowing.

Last night we saw the Northern Lights. We often see them in winter. They look like green shapes that move slowly across the sky.

My mom made some Inuit boots for you! We mailed them today. I hope you like them.

Yours truly,
Akiak

You can see the Northern Lights most clearly in the Arctic.

Look at my snow castle!

Dan
Northern Territory, Australia
To: Isabel

Hi, Isabel,

Yesterday, I fell off my horse and hurt my leg. My mom called the Royal Flying Doctor Service. The doctor arrived by airplane in just one hour. Now I have a bandage on my leg. I will be better soon. We are lucky to have Flying Doctors in the outback!

This evening we are having a barbecue. Yum!

Talk to you soon,
Dan

The Royal Flying Doctor Service is so important that its founder is on our $20 bills!

The Royal Flying Doctor Service helps people who live a long way from hospitals.

Barbecues are very popular in Australia!

Isabel

I have learned so much from my new friends! Miss Thomson asked me to write about some things I have learned.

Some of my friends live very far from a city. Others live in big cities like mine. Our favorite foods, activities, and the things we do for fun are different. The weather is different in each country. But we have lots of things in common too. We all have to do school work, and we all like to have fun. There are exciting things to do in all four places.

I can't wait to learn more about other kids from all over the world!

Glossary

caribou   type of deer

cricket   sport played with a bat and a ball and two teams of 11 players

Inuit   group of people from northern Canada and parts of Greenland and Alaska

outback   remote and rural parts of Australia

smog   pollution in the air caused by cars and factories

Index